PATHFINDER EDITION

By Nancy-Jo Hereford

CONTENTS

Voices
for
Justice

By Nancy-Jo Hereford

Dr. Martin Luther King Jr. speaks to news reporters. Television news helped people around the country understand the goals of the civil rights movement.

PRINT, photographs, television, Internet: each of these types of media inform and entertain. Together, they help us have fun, learn, and communicate with others. But from the distant past to the up-to-the-minute present, various kinds of media have been used for an additional purpose. Media has helped to support, inspire, and even inflame movements for social justice.

Think about it. Where would America be without the *Declaration of Independence* and other documents that made the case for liberty? How do photos and television images of people demanding equality and human rights help to fight injustice? How has modern social media gone from saying LOL to demanding FREEDOM NOW?

Discover how media, in one form or another, has always been a voice for justice.

IMAGINE THE WORLD of 1776, when the American Revolution was beginning. There was no telephone, television, radio, or Internet. The ways that news and **opinion** travel today had not been invented. Yet patriots rallied one another to the **cause** for independence. Their forms of communication were public speeches and, even more so, essays and arguments in writing. A common way of sharing ideas with a wide audience was to print them in a pamphlet.

A pamphlet is like a short book. It has a soft cover and is made up of sheets of paper that are stitched or stapled together. At the time of the Revolution, political pamphlets were popular reading. They were fast and cheap to produce and sold for pennies.

The most famous pamphlet is *Common Sense* by Thomas Paine. It was 46 pages and published in January 1776, seven months before the *Declaration of Independence*. Paine's title hints at how he wrote. He used plain language to explain why freedom from England made sense for America. Paine blamed the English monarch, King George III, for the unjust treatment of the colonies. He argued that the colonists should demand more than the **right** to have their own representatives in the British government. They should form their own government and become an independent country.

Common Sense became a best-seller. More than 100,000 copies were printed. As more and more colonists read and discussed Paine's ideas, their ideas changed, too. It's a big leap to imagine forming your own country. *Common Sense* helped many colonists to make that leap.

Pamphlets were a voice for justice. They gave American colonists good reasons to fight for independence and the chance to create a more fair government.

Thomas Paine wrote many pamphlets urging people to keep fighting for independence.

COMMON SENSE:
ADDRESSED TO THE
INHABITANTS
OF
AMERICA,
On the following interesting
SUBJECTS.

I. Of the Origin and Design of Government in general, with concise Remarks on the English Constitution.
II. Of Monarchy and Hereditary Succession.
III. Thoughts on the present State of American Affairs.
IV. Of the present Ability of America, with some miscellaneous Reflections.

Written by an ENGLISHMAN.
By Thomas Paine

Man knows no Master save creating HEAVEN,
Or those whom choice and common good ordain.
THOMSON.

PHILADELPHIA, Printed
And Sold by R. BELL, in Third-Street, 1776.

In Common Sense, *Paine argued that America had the resources to be independent.*

Frederick Douglass described the evils of slavery in his newspaper The North Star.

William Lloyd Garrison wanted the North to form a country with no enslavement.

Media: Abolitionist Newspapers
THE FREEDOM PRESS

WHEN YOU VIEW the American Revolution through the lens of social justice, you see both a success and a failure. With independence, the United States of America became a democratic country. But independence did not mean freedom for all. Slavery was still allowed in the new nation.

Over time, as states in the North outlawed slavery, a **movement** grew to abolish, or end, enslavement everywhere in the country. However, the abolitionist movement did not gain followers overnight. Although many people in the North did not agree with slavery, they also did not want to fight against it.

The abolitionists did not give up. They believed strongly that slavery was wrong and that they could persuade people in both the North and the South to agree with them. One way that abolitionists spread their views was through their own newspapers. Anti-slavery newspapers carried articles about the cruel treatment of enslaved people and why slavery should be abolished. Both African Americans and whites wrote and read abolitionist papers.

The Liberator was one of the best-known abolitionist newspapers. Its founder, William Lloyd Garrison, was a radical abolitionist. He once burned a copy of the U.S. Constitution because it did not ban slavery. In spite of this, people read his Boston-based newspaper for 34 years. Garrison published *The Liberator* until 1865, when the 13th Amendment abolished slavery in the United States.

Newspapers were a voice for justice. Over many years, these publications kept the goal of freedom for enslaved people in the public eye. They helped bring about a United States where there is liberty for all races.

This photo shows the 1913 march in Washington, D.C. More than 5,000 women joined the parade on Pennsylvania Avenue.

Media: Photographs
WOMEN ON THE MARCH

WHEN YOU IMAGINE America's beginning and the work of the Founding Fathers, you might also wonder if the country had Founding Mothers. Women were there, of course, but the Constitution did not give women the right to vote. In that time, women did not have the same rights as men.

This began to change in the 1800s, as women pushed for more rights. They made gains, such as getting better access to basic education. However, women's demand for suffrage, or voting rights, took a long time to win. In fact, it took 72 years.

Also during the 1800s, camera technology improved. By the late 1800s, photos could be printed in newspapers. At about the same time, suffrage leaders realized that their cause needed to get more attention. And newspaper photographs helped women's suffrage get attention. Women staged public demonstrations. They marched in city streets. They protested at the gates of the White House. And photographers captured those images for the newspapers.

The most famous suffrage march took place in Washington, D.C., in 1913. A crowd of men who were against women's suffrage got unruly, and marchers were injured. Photographers from national newspapers snapped pictures of the entire event.

The photos and newspaper stories stirred both respect for the women's fight for suffrage and outrage at what happened to those women. The Washington police chief was fired for not protecting the marchers. The march was a turning point for the suffrage campaign. It took another seven years of protest, but finally in 1920, the 19th Amendment gave all women the right to vote.

Photographs were another voice for justice. Those photos conveyed the determination of women who would not give up until they could vote!

TELEVISION is so much a part of life today, it seems like it's been around forever. But if you have great-grandparents or grandparents who were born in the 1940s or earlier, they probably did not grow up with television.

In the U.S., people first began buying television sets around 1950. By 1960, 90 percent of homes had a TV. Just as they do today, people watched to be entertained. They also watched to get the news.

Before television, people listened to news on the radio. When they went to the movies, short "newsreels" showed scenes of news events. Television news was different. It allowed people to see events in their own living rooms, day after day.

Starting in the mid-1950s, television news frequently showed African Americans in Southern cities protesting for civil rights. Some scenes were inspiring, such as hundreds of peaceful marchers gathering together. Yet many scenes of civil rights protests were ugly and violent. Viewers saw angry white adults screaming at African American children trying to attend all-white schools. They saw helpless protesters being attacked.

Remember the abolitionist newspapers that educated people about the evils of slavery? Television had a similar impact on many people around the country. Television cameras made people aware of the injustices that African Americans lived with.

Television about civil rights was a voice for justice. It helped turn public opinion in favor of national laws, passed by Congress in 1964 and 1965, to guarantee civil rights for people of all races.

Many people were able to watch Dr. Martin Luther King Jr.'s speeches on television.

Media: Documentary
CHANGING PUBLIC OPINION

THERE ARE different kinds of news and reporting. News programs, like the evening news, inform viewers. They present facts about current events. There is also another kind of current-events program called a documentary. It documents, or records, information about real events in a way that supports a particular opinion. A documentary informs viewers about a subject and tries to persuade them to care about it. Often a documentary uncovers a hidden injustice.

One television documentary that made history was broadcast one day after Thanksgiving in 1960. Remember that by 1960, most families in the U.S. had a television at home. You can imagine that many people had enjoyed a big holiday meal the day before. They were ready to relax in front of the TV.

Viewers of the documentary called "Harvest of Shame" got a jolt that eventually carried all the way to the halls of Congress. "Harvest of Shame" was about migrant farmworkers in Florida. The program revealed that these workers, who traveled from farm to farm picking crops, barely made enough money to live. Viewers were able to see their poverty and poor health.

Before "Harvest of Shame," most Americans didn't know much about the lives of migrant farmworkers. What they learned by watching the documentary caused many to demand help for these men and women. In 1962, Congress passed legislation to provide migrant farmworkers with services such as health care. That same year, Cesar Chavez organized the National Farm Workers Association in California to push for better working conditions for farm laborers.

Documentaries are another voice for justice. A successful documentary doesn't just report facts about a topic. It makes people think about their ideas and opinions. Even better, it prods them to take action to help others.

Now and in the Future

FAST-FORWARD to today. Print, photographs, television news, and documentaries are all ways that people learn about social problems. These forms of **media** are still weapons for fighting injustice. What other types of media can you name? How do they act as voices for fairness? Keep your eyes and ears open for new forms of media that ensure justice will always have a voice!

Wordwise

cause: an aim that some people support or fight for

media: ways to communicate with a wide audience, like newspapers, magazines, radio, and television

movement: people with the same beliefs or ideas who work together for change

opinion: what someone thinks about something

right: a thing you are allowed to do by law

How to Read a Web Page

Where do *you* look first to get information? Chances are you use your computer or smart phone to go to the Internet. And that's where you can find thousands of Web pages devoted to causes for social justice.

Anyone can create a page that supports a cause. So how do you know if the information you get is accurate? Like with any other source, you need to think critically. Test your critical thinking skills with this imaginary Web page for a social justice group. Decide if this is information you would trust.

Name: *Do you recognize the name?*

URL: *Is this group an organization? Connected with a university? Part of a government agency?*

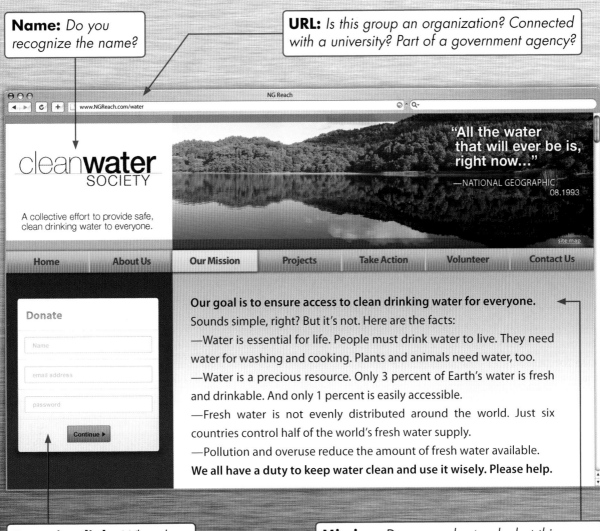

Donation link: *What does the group want visitors to do? How will donations be used?*

Mission: *Do you understand what this group is trying to accomplish? What evidence does the group use to support its ideas?*

Friending
JUSTICE

TAKE A LOOK AT JUSTICE IN THE 21ST CENTURY.

"Tweeting" Revolution

In the early 21st century, social media has changed the way friends and family members stay in touch with each other. People talk, text, and send photographs from anywhere with their cell phones. They connect with others they choose to "friend" on personal Web pages. They post videos that may be serious or silly on the Internet. They follow the goings-on of pals and even celebrities with 140-character "tweets."

Revolutionary Media

These types of social media were developed as communication tools. Compared with forms of communication in the past, social media is revolutionary. And in some places in the world, it is being used to spread revolution, too.

Around the globe, people struggle to gain more political and personal freedom. Where people have access to social media, it has become a force for freedom. Protest leaders can "tweet" thousands at once with critical news. They can snap a photo with a cell phone and send it in seconds to inform or rally supporters. Controlling information is one of the ways that unjust leaders stay in power. Social media enables people to get the real truth about problems out to the world before unjust governments can stop them.

A woman waves the flag of Egypt. Notice the people taking photos with their cell phones.

Protesting Online and in the Street

A revolution in Egypt in 2011 is an example of the impact of social media. President Hosni Mubarak was forced to resign after ruling Egypt for thirty years. To stay in power, his government tried to stop dissent, or disagreement. Through social media, people found a way to share their views. One group, called the April 6 Youth Movement, used a Web page to organize protests and gain members who agreed with their demands for free speech and other rights.

Protests against President Mubarak brought together thousands of Egyptians of all ages. "Tweets" and texting helped keep information flowing. The protests continued to build until it was clear the Egyptian people demanded a new, more democratic leader. President Mubarak stepped down.

Printed Pages to Texted "Tweets"

Social media was not developed to spread revolution. But then, television wasn't invented to support the civil rights movement. Cameras weren't created just to capture images of protests and marches. Newspapers and other publications, both now and in the past, are not printed only to educate readers about injustice in the world.

However, people who fight against inequality and unfairness are resourceful. They find the tools they need to expose prejudice and wrong-doing. They find ways to help create a better, brighter world. From printed pages to texted "tweets" to what follows in the future, media has always been a friend to justice.

MediaMessages

Spread the message. Answer these
questions about media and justice.

 1 How did people communicate
their ideas and opinions during
the American Revolution?

 2 Why was photography important for
the women's suffrage movement?

3 How did television change the way
people got news?

4 List three things to consider when
you look at a Web page.

5 How are the ways people use
media to spread social justice
today different from in the past?